THE
WORKING RELATIONSHIPS
POCKETBOOK

By Fiona Elsa Dent

Drawings by Phil Hailstone

"The world of work has rightly turned its attention to relati........... ....
the relationship with oneself and with others, both personally and professionally, is at the hub of a
fulfilling life. When these relationships are fruitful, there is dynamic movement and progress.
When there is difficulty, the resulting dilemmas can provide the route map for the changes needed.
This book provides a valuable outworking of some of these principles and I commend it to you."
Philippa Morrison, Faculty and Senior Staff Development Advisor, London Business School

Published by:
Management Pocketbooks Ltd
Laurel House, Station Approach, Alresford, Hants SO24 9JH, U.K.
Tel: +44 (0)1962 735573   Fax: +44 (0)1962 733637
E-mail: sales@pocketbook.co.uk
Website: www.pocketbook.co.uk

This edition published 2009

© Fiona Elsa Dent 2009

British Library Cataloguing-in-Publication Data. A catalogue record for this book is available from the British Library.

ISBN 978 1 903776 97 1

Design, typesetting and graphics by **efex ltd**. Printed in U.K.

CONTENTS

THANKS FROM THE AUTHOR

I'd like to express my thanks to:

- All the participants on the many development programmes where relationship issues have been discussed, who have helped me formulate my thoughts and ideas

- All the people who took part in my research and helped contribute to the ideas expressed in this book

- My colleagues at Ashridge who work with me on the Creating Working Relationships Programme

- Jan for helping with proof reading and sense making

- My family, who provide me with my best 'working' relationship

1

INTRODUCTION

SOCIAL BEINGS

'Consider the following. We humans are social beings. We come into the world as the result of others' actions. We survive here in dependence on others. Whether we like it or not, there is hardly a moment of our lives when we do not benefit from others' activities. For this reason it is hardly surprising that most of our happiness arises in the context of our relationships with others.'

The Dalai Lama

IMPROVING THE SOFT SKILLS

21st century organisations require 21st century skills and abilities. Ongoing research undertaken at the Centre for Creative Leadership suggests that one of the emerging distinguishing features of success will be higher awareness of, and improved ability in, the so called 'soft skills'. One area that requires these soft skills, and consistently emerges as a challenge for today's leaders and managers, is that of developing and managing effective work based relationships.

Awareness of this led me to embark upon a research project to help me understand more about how and why people create relationships, what they do to sustain them, what makes these relationships succeed and what makes them go wrong. To gather the data I used a variety of techniques including a questionnaire, interviews and focus groups.

The book suggests ideas, knowledge, tools and techniques that will help people in organisations better understand what's necessary to be successful in this complex and often messy area.

WHO THIS BOOK IS FOR

The focus of the book is on helping you to recognise and identify your own approach to relationships at work. By doing this you will, in turn, become better able to identify and understand the differences in other people's approaches and modify your own behaviour accordingly. It is this modification, allied to good interpersonal and communication skills that will allow you to improve your relationships.

The book is intended for:

● Any person working in any type of organisation who wants to know more about how to make the best of their work based relationships

● People who want to understand more about their own approach to relationships at work and to learn some tips and techniques to help them improve their interpersonal skills

People who wish to explore, develop, and be more effective in any relationship, whether at work or elsewhere, might also find it useful.

INTRODUCTION

WHAT IT COVERS

The book is **not** intended to be a manual for handling bullies or dealing with serious workplace conflict. It **is** about the range of interpersonal skills that contribute to effective relationship management and it may, therefore, help you understand elements of these difficult relationships and provide you with ideas for making improvements.

It will encourage you to reflect on the range and quality of your work based relationships and offer tips, techniques and ideas to help you develop and improve them.

The first half of the book focuses on self-reflection and asks you to consider:

- Why you create relationships
- What makes you develop and sustain relationships
- Your relationship style

The second part of the book examines features and tools that you can apply to your relationship approach.

TYPICAL PROBLEM AREAS

These are some of the typical reasons people give for wanting to develop and improve their relationship management skills:

- To help deal with people problems at work
- To help manage relationships with the boss/colleagues/reports
- To deal more effectively with 'difficult' people
- To increase confidence and skill
- To help get things done
- To cope with organisational and office politics
- To be a more effective leader
- To manage change more effectively
- To understand the skills, techniques and approaches for successful interpersonal relationships

TYPICAL PROBLEM AREAS

> *'The No 1 factor for derailment is poor interpersonal skills – our inability to get along with people.'*
> **John Alexander (President of the Centre for Creative Leadership)**

Personal reflection

Think about the following two questions regarding your own work based relationships:

- What relationship challenges do I face?
- Why do I want to develop my relationship skills?

DEFINITION OF A WORKING RELATIONSHIP

The term 'working relationship' refers to those relationships you develop at work that contribute to your success and effectiveness in the working environment.

> It is:
>
> 'Any productive, open and honest relationship where both parties feel they can contribute in an atmosphere of mutuality.'

CREATING RELATIONSHIPS

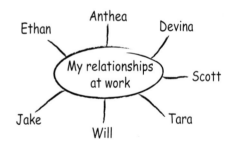

CREATING RELATIONSHIPS

UNDERSTAND YOUR RELATIONSHIPS

The first step in your quest to improve your relationships at work is to have a full understanding of the current range of your relationships. The following practical exercise will provide you with a visual expression of this.

Exercise: Map your network

1. Create a network map illustrating the people you relate with at work. See the example – though for most people there will be rather more than seven colleagues on it, so your map will be a little more complex.

2. Reflect on your map and think about the reasons **you** create relationships at work.

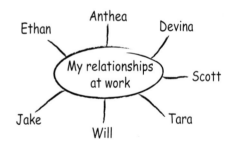

WHY WE START RELATIONSHIPS

The research literature and my own conclusions, drawn from conversation with colleagues and training participants, both throw up three key reasons why people start work based relationships:

1. Part of the work team – people are thrown together and therefore have to form some sort of relationship.

2. For functional reasons – you develop a relationship because it is necessary for greater effectiveness in your work.

3. For social reasons – you develop a personal or emotional attachment.

CREATING RELATIONSHIPS

1. PART OF THE WORK TEAM

Who
- The boss
- People you manage
- Team members/colleagues

Why
- It's part of the job description to develop relationships with fellow team members
- It's necessary for work based in the department

The people in your work team are usually the people you work most closely with. They are also those you have least choice about. As a manager on one of our courses said:

> *'These relationships are all superficial and often easy to let go.'*

While this may be the case, it is always best for all concerned to have good working relationships with work team colleagues. Taking time to get to know each person and establish an effective relationship with them is valuable in the long run.

CREATING RELATIONSHIPS

2. FUNCTIONAL RELATIONSHIPS

hello!

Who
- People you have to have a relationship with, because you work with them on various tasks, projects, committees, etc
- People working in other functions who could be of use to you

Why
- Entirely based round work
- To gain respect for the work you do
- To get the job done
- Targeting people for their expertise
- The network culture in the organisation

These relationships are transactional and time-bound, based on necessity to get the job done. As one manager pointed out:

> *'These are relationships developed purely for transactional reasons, and when the usefulness is over they are easily forgotten.'*

Yet, they still have to work effectively while they are necessary and are worth nurturing afterwards – just in case!

3. SOCIAL RELATIONSHIPS

Who
- People you like or who are like you
- Someone you have instant rapport with

Why
- A desire to develop more social relationships
- You have something in common
- You get on well and make a connection

These relationships are made with people you choose to spend time with and may well be with people from outside your own department or work area – those whom you relate to more easily. To quote a participant:

'In this type of relationship choice plays a major role and an emotional attachment or connection is made.'

CREATING RELATIONSHIPS

WHERE DO YOUR RELATIONSHIPS FIT?

Going back to your network map of work based relationships, categorise each person within the three areas:

Part of the work team	For work or functional reasons	For social reasons

ANOTHER WAY TO CATEGORISE

A slightly different approach to the categorisation of your work based relationships would be to think in terms of acquaintances, colleagues and your inner circle.

- **Acquaintances** – people you know at work, with whom you are reasonably friendly, chatting about superficial topics, but with whom you have little day to day work contact. You may not know much about these people and almost certainly they will not be central to your success in your role

- **Colleagues** – those people you spend time with each day, with a reasonable level of work involvement, and who have some degree of impact upon your effectiveness and success in your job

- **Inner circle** – extremely close work colleagues on whom you depend at both an emotional and work based level. You will probably know a lot about them and will often use them as a sounding board. They may or may not have a direct impact on your success in your job but, because of your relationship with them, you know they will have impact on you personally as you trust and respect their judgement

PERSONAL REFLECTION

Using the categories described on the previous page, plot your relationships onto a chart similar to the following:

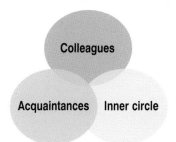

Now reflect upon the messages this may be conveying to you about the various people in your relationship network:

- Which category are most of your relationships in?

- Are your relationships spread evenly between categories?

- What patterns can you see, for instance:
  – Where do you place your work colleagues?
  – Where are the people senior to you?
  – Where are the people who report to you?

We are all different – there is no typical pattern. The important thing is to be aware of your own pattern and what it tells you about your work based relationships.

CREATING RELATIONSHIPS

PERSONAL REFLECTION

Looking back at the different ways of categorising work relationships, you can then ask yourself whether there are any overlaps between:

- Acquaintances & Part of work team
- Colleagues & Functional relationships
- Inner circle & Social relationships

What insights can you gain from this data? For instance:

- What messages might you be conveying to others about the importance of different groups of people in your relationship network?
- Are many of your work team and functional colleagues in your inner circle?
- Who do you tend to develop inner circle/social relationships with?

DEVELOPING & SUSTAINING RELATIONSHIPS

EMOTIONAL CONNECTION

It appears that relationships at work are not immune from the rules that apply elsewhere, ie that for relationships to develop and grow, a personal or emotional connection needs to be established, usually through having **something in common**, either at work or socially.

It is clear that personal or emotional attachment is of particular importance in establishing quality relationships that are mutually beneficial and rewarding. Relationships developed purely for work based reasons can be useful but, not surprisingly, tend to be more transient and less long lasting.

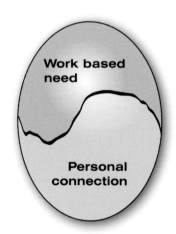

Work based need

Personal connection

4-BOX MODEL

Combining the personal/emotional aspect with the work based transactional need, leads us to a model of work based relationships that suggests four basic approaches to relationships at work:

- Casual
- Transactional
- Social
- Mutually dependent

These approaches are all possible ways of relating to others.

4-BOX MODEL

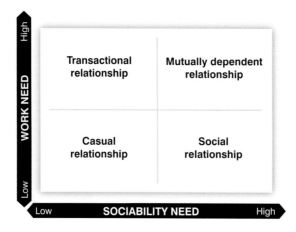

DEVELOPING & SUSTAINING RELATIONSHIPS

4-BOX MODEL EXPLAINED

Casual relationships (low work need, low sociability need) – these relationships are not relevant to core activities and are therefore peripheral and superficial.

Social relationships (low work need, high sociability need) – the main motivation for the relationship is the existence of an emotional connection which leads to friendliness.

Transactional relationships (high work need, low sociability need) – these are professional relationships necessary to get a job done.

Mutually dependent relationships (high work need, high sociability need) – these are the most productive and valuable work relationships.

EXAMPLES

Transactional relationship – Someone with whom you must work to get the job done but not a natural friend, more often a person you are thrown together with on a project.

Mutually dependent relationship – Respect and enjoyment are key in this type of relationship. You choose to work and socialise with these people: you are on the same wavelength.

Casual relationship – Someone you encounter regularly and exchange pleasantries with, eg the receptionist, security staff, a senior manager from another department, etc.

Social relationship – The person you turn to in challenging times: you share ideas, moans and groans, gossip and actively choose to spend work social time together.

PERSONAL REFLECTION

Stage 1
Draw a copy of the chart (without the names/scores in our example) and make a list of all your current relationships. Now analyse them and decide for each person the level of work and social need that applies to them.

Name	Work need	Social need
	Score on a scale of 1 – low to 10 – high	
Ben	7	3
Sonja	3	9
Garth	9	8
Marc	4	6
Alex	1	2

PERSONAL REFLECTION

Stage 2
Plotting your relationships on to the model:

- Draw a chart on a sheet of paper

- Mark each relationship on the chart (see example here)

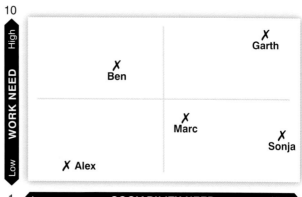

ANALYSIS OF THE CHART

Typically, one would expect to see a spread of relationships throughout the four boxes. While the spread may not be even, most of us should have relationships in each box.

What does this information tell you? Questions you may like to consider:

- Are you happy with the scatter of the relationships?

- Are there any relationships you would like to move from one box to another? How might you do this? (Try out some of the techniques later in this book.)

- What does the overall pattern tell you about your attitude to relationships at work?

- Do you think the other people would position your relationship with them in the same place? If not, why not, and how might this affect your relationship?

DEVELOPING & SUSTAINING RELATIONSHIPS

CASE STUDY 1 – JIM

Jim is an engineer working for a small manufacturing company where he has been for several years. His role as a design engineer is his dream job. Jim likes working on his own, managing his own workload and reporting to his boss as and when necessary. His boss trusts him to get on with the job and that's the way Jim likes it.

Jim says that he doesn't like to depend on anyone else and doesn't like anyone to depend on him. His job is quite detailed and he likes to focus on this detail and work independently. He has always prided himself on being efficient and self-reliant. However, while this has worked well for him for many years, things are changing. His organisation has recently taken on a new managing director with very different ideas.

C
A
S
E

S
T
U
D
Y

DEVELOPING & SUSTAINING RELATIONSHIPS

CASE STUDY 1 – JIM

The new boss wants people to work in teams, share ideas, take part in performance reviews and attend training courses! It was on a training course that I met Jim. He had been asked to attend because he wasn't adapting well to the new regime and this was causing problems back at work. Jim explained that he still loved his job, but the new culture at work had changed everything.

During the course Jim identified that his preferred relationship style was very practical, and he was strongly task focused and reserved. He related to all the positive elements of this style and agreed that some of the drawbacks – specifically, his impersonal, formal, unemotional approach – were now holding him back in the new regime.

CASE STUDY 1 – JIM

He also identified that most of his relationships at work were casual, with a few edging into transactional. He had never felt the need to get close to people at work; all his social relationships were with people outside work.

While Jim admitted that it was not his choice to come on the course, he wanted to work things out and understand how to fit in better. Being more relationship oriented was clearly something he needed for future effectiveness and continued success in his job.

During the course Jim tried out some new relationship approaches (these included: asking more questions at meetings, offering opinions and support to others, joining others for lunch occasionally). He began reviewing his current work situation and relationships. We developed an action plan focusing on small steps Jim could take to adopt some of the behaviours necessary to adapt to the new way of working.

DEVELOPING & SUSTAINING RELATIONSHIPS

CASE STUDY 1 – JIM

JIM'S ACTION POINTS

- To draw up a relationship network map of his current work based relationships and use this as a basis for analysis, in order to identify which relationships were most necessary and valuable and, therefore, where to focus his initial efforts

- To include on the map, in addition to existing relationships, those people he felt he needed to get to know better

- To join others for lunch at least once a week

- To coach some of the new engineering staff

- To be more involved in team meetings by asking questions and offering thoughts, views and ideas

- To discuss all this with his immediate boss and ask for support and feedback on progress

From the toolkit (see final chapter), aspects of **impression management**, **skilful dialogue** and **feedback** would be useful for Jim's continued development.

ONE MAIN INGREDIENT

'The most important single ingredient in the formula of success is knowing how to get along with people.'

Theodore Roosevelt

RELATIONSHIP STYLE

INTRODUCTION

So far we have looked at your approaches to creating, developing and sustaining relationships. We now move on to a model that examines relationship style, another significant factor in how you relate to others.

Most of us have a preferred relationship style. This means that typically you adopt a favoured range of skills and behaviours when interacting with others. These behaviours and skills, taken together, define your particular relationship style. Understanding your typical style can help you to see why it is easier to create and sustain certain relationships with some people than with others.

There are many ways of looking at relationship style – some well known models include: Myers-Briggs Type Indicator®, Relationship Awareness Theory® and Social Style Model™. The model on the following page uses two orientations which contribute to the way we relate to others.

MODEL

People focus

Reserved ← → **Outgoing**

Task focus

RELATIONSHIP STYLE

MODEL EXPLAINED

This particular model of relationship style looks at two orientations – People/Task and Reserved/Outgoing.

- People/Task is about where your focus lies – are you primarily people focused or task focused?
- Reserved/Outgoing is about how you relate to the external world – are you more introverted or more extroverted?

Both orientations play a part in the way you relate to others and how you are perceived by others in terms of your relationship style. Within these two orientations four different styles can be identified.

THE FOUR STYLES

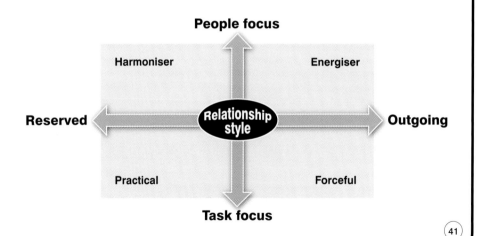

People focus

Harmoniser

Energiser

Reserved

Relationship style

Outgoing

Practical

Forceful

Task focus

IDENTIFYING YOUR STYLE

Look at the statements below and rank the statements in each row from 1 to 4 (with 1 being the statement most like you and 4 the statement least like you). If in doubt about the answer, think specifically about your behaviour in the workplace rather than at home.

☐ I like to be of support to others	☐ I like to be businesslike with others	☐ I am enthusiastic in my relations with others	☐ I express my opinions openly
☐ I want to be friendly with others	☐ I need time to get to know others	☐ I like lively discussions	☐ I like to be in control in relationships
☐ I am a good listener	☐ I tend to be more formal in relationships	☐ I make relationships easily	☐ I tend to focus on action in relationships
☐ I work towards co-operative relations with others	☐ I am reserved in initiating relationships	☐ I have been described as high spirited	☐ I am influential in relationships
☐ My default position is to trust others	☐ I am dependable in relationships	☐ I get excited about possibilities when working with others	☐ I openly stand up for my views
☐ Total - A	☐ Total - B	☐ Total - C	☐ Total - D

IDENTIFYING YOUR STYLE

Reflect on the words below and rank the words in each row from 1 to 4 (with 1 the word most like you and 4 the one least like you). As before, it is your workplace personality that is relevant.

☐ Harmony	☐ Practical	☐ Energetic	☐ Powerful
☐ Collaborative	☐ Realistic	☐ Lively	☐ Strong
☐ Open	☐ Sensible	☐ Active	☐ Influential
☐ Co-operative	☐ Reasonable	☐ Animated	☐ Persuasive
☐ Supportive	☐ Rational	☐ Bubbly	☐ Convincing
☐ Obliging	☐ Equitable	☐ Spirited	☐ Compelling
☐ Accommodating	☐ Level-headed	☐ Passionate	☐ Dominant
☐ Helpful	☐ Logical	☐ Cheerful	☐ Competitive
☐ Caring	☐ Consistent	☐ Dynamic	☐ Demanding
☐ Kind	☐ Dependable	☐ Vibrant	☐ Challenging

Total - A	Total - B	Total - C	Total - D

IDENTIFYING YOUR STYLE

ANALYSING YOUR RESPONSES

Transfer the totals from pages 42 and 43 into the table below:

	Column A	Column B	Column C	Column D
Page 42				
Page 43				
Total				
Style	Harmoniser	Practical	Energiser	Forceful
Order of preference lowest to highest				

My preferred style (the one with the lowest score) is

My least preferred style (the one with the highest score) is

STYLE OVERVIEW

People focus

HARMONISERS are people oriented. They want to be of support to others and to develop open, friendly and trusting relationships.

ENERGISERS are fast paced, enthusiastic and outgoing. They develop relationships based on intuition, vision and trust.

Reserved ← Relationship style → **Outgoing**

PRACTICAL people are organised, businesslike and efficient. They want relationships where information, facts and evidence feature.

FORCEFUL people want results oriented relationships where speed and control feature.

Task focus

STYLE CHARACTERISTICS

When working at their best, these are the characteristics of each style:

People focus

HARMONISERS
Amiable	Warm
Collaborative	Open
Supportive	Friendly
Quiet	Listener
Co-operative	Patient

ENERGISERS
Inspirational	Creative
Excitable	Enthusiastic
Intuitive	Lively
Chatty	Passionate
High-spirited	Influential

Reserved ← **Relationship style** → **Outgoing**

PRACTICAL
Orderly	Precise
Organised	Structured
Thorough	Efficient
Conservative	Systematic
Businesslike	Factual

FORCEFUL
Assertive	Confident
Initiator	Directive
Decisive	Action-oriented
Challenging	Controlling
Opinionated	Results-oriented

Task focus

STYLE CHARACTERISTICS

When at their worst, each style can be seen as:

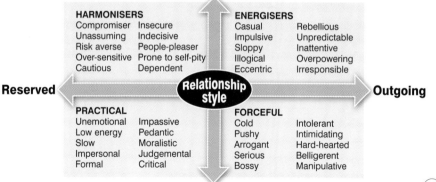

People focus

Reserved ← → **Outgoing**

Relationship style

HARMONISERS

Compromiser	Insecure
Unassuming	Indecisive
Risk averse	People-pleaser
Over-sensitive	Prone to self-pity
Cautious	Dependent

ENERGISERS

Casual	Rebellious
Impulsive	Unpredictable
Sloppy	Inattentive
Illogical	Overpowering
Eccentric	Irresponsible

PRACTICAL

Unemotional	Impassive
Low energy	Pedantic
Slow	Moralistic
Impersonal	Judgemental
Formal	Critical

FORCEFUL

Cold	Intolerant
Pushy	Intimidating
Arrogant	Hard-hearted
Serious	Belligerent
Bossy	Manipulative

Task focus

47

RELATIONSHIP STYLE

PERSONAL REFLECTION

My preferred relationship style is ………………..

Questions to consider:

- How appropriate and successful is this style for my current work based relationships?
- What are the advantages of using this style for my current relationships?
- What are the disadvantages/challenges?
- What can I learn from the other styles?
- Which style might help me be even more successful as a relationship manager?
- What can I do to develop skill in using this style in my relationships?

WORKING WITH OTHERS

Your relationship style describes your preferred approach to managing your work based relationships. This style will have an impact on how you are perceived by others and how others treat you in their relationships with you.

Usually, a person will react to others in a way that makes them feel comfortable themselves. Like so many things we do in life, our immediate natural response is habitual and focuses primarily on our own comfort. Unfortunately this can mean that we treat everyone the same, leading to misunderstanding and awkwardness in many relationships.

If you can put yourself in the other person's shoes and relate to them in a manner that matches the way they want to be treated, you are likely to have more productive and better quality working relationships.

WORKING WITH OTHERS

Modifying your style to match that of others involves:

- Observing their behaviour and relationship patterns to identify their preferred way of working – their relationship style
- Identifying, from their own style, what behaviours and approaches you might use to make them feel more comfortable and create a more productive relationship
- Ensuring that you come across as authentic when adopting new behaviours

Sounds easy? Remember, old habits die hard!

It will take time, effort and practice to develop the capability to adapt and flex your usual behaviour to relate more effectively to others. Research has shown that small changes in behaviour to match and relate to others will lead to big pay offs in relationships and in performance as a leader and manager.

MATCHING STYLES

- Think about a person in your relationship network who makes you feel uncomfortable
- Reflect and make notes on the person's behaviour patterns (eg: body language, vocal usage, general impression created) and your perception of their relationship style
- Identify what you feel you could do differently in the way you relate to them to make the relationship more effective
- Now try it out
- Reflect on any changes in their response to you

Ask for feedback.

Remember, relating to others is not just about reacting, it's also about adapting.

CASE STUDY 2 – SANJOY

Sanjoy attended one of our training courses and initially we wondered why he was there. It became clearer as the workshop progressed. During a short coaching session, Sanjoy explained that although he generally had good relationships at work, occasionally he found that people reacted quite negatively to him. Sanjoy liked to have open and friendly relationships with his work colleagues, describing himself as upbeat, positive, always ready to look on the bright side. He disliked confrontation and did all he could to avoid it.

He gave, as an example, a recent conversation with a colleague, Sue. They had worked together for nine months and generally got on well. On this particular occasion (and it was typical of similar responses he had had from others, men and women) Sue had reacted badly. In a fairly normal example of office chit chat, Sue had been telling him about a problem she was experiencing with their boss. *(The particular issue is unimportant here – what is relevant is Sanjoy's way of relating to Sue during the interaction.)*

CASE STUDY 2 – SANJOY

While Sanjoy empathised with Sue, he didn't want to get too involved as he always found it difficult to offer advice and solutions for relationship problems. So he made light of the issue, teased her a bit and suggested that if she left well alone the problem would go away. Sue's response was unexpected – she told Sanjoy he was really unsympathetic, making her feel that her problem was unimportant and that she was over-reacting.

Sanjoy was upset about this and went on to explain that this was not the first time someone had accused him of not empathising. He found this particularly distressing as he saw himself as outgoing and friendly – an energiser in style. He enjoyed having social relationships with his workmates and had thought that most of his relationships were mutually dependent.

CASE STUDY 2 – SANJOY

As we explored his interaction with Sue in greater depth, Sanjoy came to realise that there was a pattern to his behaviour when in conversations about people's relationship problems. He simply didn't like giving relationship advice and wanted to avoid this type of conversation. He had therefore developed a way of coping that he thought kept people happy, while leaving him feeling comfortable that he'd listened and been a friend. Clearly this was not always the case.

This led to a discussion of the energiser style. Sanjoy recognised that when people chatted to him about their 'problems' he sometimes appeared to discount them by using humour and quickly suggesting a solution. Energisers can sometimes appear a little casual and inattentive; depending on the other person's relationship needs and style this behaviour can be seen as offhand and dismissive.

Sanjoy began to understand what was going wrong. He now wanted to plan how to remedy the situation with Sue. He also needed to work out a way of being able to listen to similar problems without feeling too uncomfortable or appearing dismissive.

C
A
S
E

S
T
U
D
Y

RELATIONSHIP STYLE

CASE STUDY 2 – SANJOY

SANJOY'S ACTION POINTS

- To understand that sometimes people just want someone to listen – not to offer solutions, simply to listen

- To develop a process for himself that involves listening to the other person and then using questions to encourage them to explore the issue for themselves

- To follow that by either summarising what he thinks they have said or asking them to summarise what they feel now and/or what they are going to do

- To be prepared to say if he feels the issue is too personal, explaining that he doesn't think he is the right person to help on this occasion, and perhaps suggesting someone better suited

C
A
S
E

S
T
U
D
Y

CASE STUDY 2 – SANJOY

SANJOY'S ACTION POINTS

- To apologise to Sue and explain where he thinks he went wrong and how he plans to be more empathetic in future – perhaps even asking her to provide occasional feedback on his progress

- To practise the **solution talk** technique and the **appreciative focus** technique (see toolkit, final chapter), both of which he felt could be useful additions to his existing approach and overcome aspects of his need to avoid confrontation

Sanjoy was unusual in that he recognised that what appeared to be a simple misunderstanding could develop into something more complex, leading to a reduction in his relationship effectiveness with others. By acting quickly and giving himself (through attending a training course) the opportunity to reflect, discuss and plan a course of action, he avoided a much longer term problem.

C
A
S
E

S
T
U
D
Y

FEATURES OF SUCCESSFUL RELATIONSHIPS

FEATURES OF SUCCESSFUL RELATIONSHIPS

INTRODUCTION

We now turn to considering the ingredients that contribute to success and effectiveness in relationships.

Based on data from a range of recent research projects and discussions with working managers, certain key features, shown on the next page, have been identified as important for success and effectiveness in relationships.

Writing in the Sunday Times, Steve Farrar said: 'The ability to relate well to other people – colleagues, staff and customers – is seen as essential to attracting and retaining talent, while its absence is blamed for high staff turnover and lost creative opportunities'.

In the same article he also says: 'Microsoft asked 500 UK business leaders what the most sought after skills were. Team working and interpersonal skills topped the list.'

Farrar S (2008) Sunday Times, 16 March

FEATURES OF SUCCESSFUL RELATIONSHIPS

RELATIONSHIP MANAGEMENT COMPETENCES

Self-focus
- Assertiveness
- Communication skills
- Caring & supporting
- Honesty & integrity
- Listening & questioning
- Self-awareness

Relationship features

Focus on others
- Awareness of others
- Building trust
- Rapport & empathy
- Emotional awareness
- Emotional management
- Mutual respect

FEATURES OF SUCCESSFUL RELATIONSHIPS

SELF-FOCUS

ASSERTIVENESS

The first quality on the list is assertiveness, valued because it involves thinking and behaving in a forthright, frank and straightforward manner so that people know where you are coming from and what you expect of them.

Characteristics of an assertive person include:
- Self-confidence in dialogue
- A self-assured confident manner and approach
- Being regarded as firm and fair by others
- Confronting issues appropriately without getting personal
- Putting own ideas across energetically
- Demonstrating clarity in thinking and action

'The basic difference between being assertive and being aggressive is how our words and behaviour affect the rights and well being of others.'
Sharon Anthony Bower (Author)

FEATURES OF SUCCESSFUL RELATIONSHIPS

SELF-FOCUS
ASSERTIVENESS

It is easy to be assertive some of the time, especially when talking about a topic well within your competence area. Sometimes, however, a relationship can be badly affected by an over-assertive approach (or indeed a painful lack of assertiveness). So, here are some ideas to help you develop and demonstrate the right level:

- Be clear what it is you want
- Make sure you have the other person's attention when communicating with them
- Say what you want – express yourself clearly, stating your views on the topic and indicating your depth of feeling
- When making suggestions, distinguish between fact and opinion
- Be aware of your language: eg use 'could' not 'should'
- Be willing to work with others to develop and explore ideas
- Tell the truth, be honest and take responsibility for your thoughts, words and actions

Assertiveness is not about winning all the time; it is about getting your point across and working with others to reach effective outcomes. (For more tips see *The Assertiveness Pocketbook*.)

FEATURES OF SUCCESSFUL RELATIONSHIPS

SELF-FOCUS
COMMUNICATION SKILLS

Communication is a huge area and there are many books dedicated to this topic alone. In terms of how communication relates to relationships, it's all about conveying ideas and information clearly and in an appropriate manner for the audience.

A good communicator selects and uses the right means of communication for the situation and people involved. There is skill involved in choosing the best channel, eg verbal, written, email or telephone. For example, there are times when a brief face to face meeting might defuse a brewing argument that an email would have exacerbated.

You also need to consider matching the message to the size of the audience: bad or unexpected news, for example, is better delivered one to one. People are invariably affected by what they think those around them might be thinking. Knowingly or unknowingly they will play to the gallery.

> *'Think like a wise man but communicate in the language of the people.'*
> **William Butler Yeats (Irish dramatist and poet 1865-1939)**

FEATURES OF SUCCESSFUL RELATIONSHIPS

SELF-FOCUS
COMMUNICATION SKILLS

Communication skills are at the heart of successful relationship management, so improving your skills in this area is vital for your confidence and success. These pointers will help you:

- Know what you want to say and how you want to say it
- Analyse and select the most appropriate communication method taking account of the person, the situation and the environment
- Practise observing others by listening with both the ears and eyes
- Look out for the cues and clues others are giving you
- Prepare your message and yourself
- Think about how you will gain the other person's attention
- Listen and question to develop a conversation and ensure mutual understanding
- Practise closing strategies: summarising, asking for action, agreeing next stage, thanks

FEATURES OF SUCCESSFUL RELATIONSHIPS

SELF-FOCUS
CARING & SUPPORTING

Many successful relationships are based on the people involved being caring and supportive of one another, showing consideration, compassion and encouragement when interacting. Some of the key characteristics of this capability include:

- Being patient and helpful when listening to others
- Showing consideration when working with others
- Being diplomatic
- Accommodating people's needs and wants
- Showing compassion and kindness when appropriate
- Demonstrating sensitivity and warmth

'Too often we underestimate the power of a touch, a smile, a kind word, a listening ear, an honest compliment, or the smallest act of caring, all of which have the potential to turn a life around.'
Leo Buscaglia (US author and lecturer, 1925-1998)

FEATURES OF SUCCESSFUL RELATIONSHIPS

SELF-FOCUS
CARING & SUPPORTING

Demonstrating and developing caring and supporting skills is largely about sensitivity – your own sensitivity to others' needs. The following ideas may help you:

- **Sincerity** – demonstrate that you care by engaging in authentic and sincere conversation, using appropriate body language and vocal tones
- **Self-disclosure** – people will sometimes feel you care more if you can share your own experiences, thoughts and feelings with them
- **Coaching and mentoring** – offer your support to others in your areas of expertise
- **Listening skills** – use encouraging gestures and vocal tones (mmm…, yes, ah ha..)
- **Being available** – take time to listen to others, even if you are not sure you can help. Maybe you can suggest someone who can
- **Show support** – stand up for people when they need your backing
- **Actions speak louder** – don't just express care and support, be willing to help out if necessary

FEATURES OF SUCCESSFUL RELATIONSHIPS

SELF-FOCUS
HONESTY & INTEGRITY

Honesty and integrity dramatically influence the quality of the relationships you have. An individual who does not display these characteristics in relationships will almost certainly have a significant majority of casual or transactional relationships that are without depth.

The qualities of honesty and integrity require you to demonstrate ethical and moral standards at work and in relationships. Your actions must be consistent with your words, and you should always keep people's confidences and be principled in what you do.

People will often use honesty and integrity as a measure of whether or not to develop a relationship with someone. They genuinely do not want people they assess as dishonest in their relationship network, except possibly at the most superficial level.

> *'Honesty is the first chapter of the book of wisdom.'*
> **Thomas Jefferson (3rd president of US, 1743-1826)**
>
> *'Honesty is like an icicle; if once it melts that is the end of it.'*
> **(Proverb)**

FEATURES OF SUCCESSFUL RELATIONSHIPS

SELF-FOCUS
HONESTY & INTEGRITY

You must be aware that people are making judgements about your behaviour all the time. Demonstrate your honesty and integrity by:

- Saying what you mean and meaning what you say – standing up for what you believe is right

- Appreciating the importance of being dependable – don't let people down

- Protecting confidentiality – when someone shares something in confidence respect their wishes. If you would find this difficult, say so

- Making realistic promises and keeping them

- Demonstrating authenticity and sincerity in all communication

- Seeking feedback from others about their perception of your honesty and integrity

- When you make a mistake admitting it and encouraging others to do the same

- If you have an ethical dilemma asking others for guidance in dealing with it

FEATURES OF SUCCESSFUL RELATIONSHIPS

SELF-FOCUS
LISTENING & QUESTIONING

Effective listening and questioning is a key communication skill and, once again, one that is vital for effective relationships. It's not just about hearing the words that are spoken, but also about being aware of the other messages the individual is conveying while speaking. You also need to demonstrate that you are listening to the whole message.

Techniques:

- Attentive listening – to the whole message, the words and the non-verbal communication, both body language and vocal usage
- Encouraging others to express themselves
- Asking incisive questions that really probe the issue and enhance your understanding
- Not interrupting
- Reflecting back to others what you have heard them say
- Clarifying and summarising to test and ensure understanding

> *'Really listening and suspending one's own judgment is necessary in order to understand other people on their own terms... This is a process that requires trust and builds trust.'*
> **Mary Field Belenky (Author and consultant on human development)**

FEATURES OF SUCCESSFUL RELATIONSHIPS

SELF-FOCUS
LISTENING & QUESTIONING

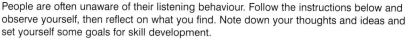

People are often unaware of their listening behaviour. Follow the instructions below and observe yourself, then reflect on what you find. Note down your thoughts and ideas and set yourself some goals for skill development.

1. Take some time to focus on your listening behaviour with different people and in different situations:

- Colleagues
- Bosses
- Different nationalities
- Younger or older
- Gender

- Formal meetings
- Group discussions
- Social settings
- One to one discussions

SELF-FOCUS
LISTENING & QUESTIONING

2. While focusing, reflect on your behaviour and notice when you fall into some of the following traps:

- Interrupting
- Becoming impatient
- Suggesting solutions before fully understanding
- Misinterpreting the message
- Talking more than listening
- Wandering off the topic – in your mind
- Planning your response and stopping listening

FEATURES OF SUCCESSFUL RELATIONSHIPS

SELF-FOCUS
LISTENING & QUESTIONING

A major element of good listening is asking good questions. It demonstrates effective listening, and also shows interest in the person and the topic under discussion.

- Use open questions to encourage the other person to talk, eg: *'Tell me about...'* *'What do you think about....?'* *'How do you feel about....?'*
- Use probing questions to encourage more information and show interest, eg: *'Anything else?'* *'Any more to add?'*
- Don't be afraid of silence between questions
- Wait before responding to a reply – there may be more to come
- Clarify to ensure you understand, testing out what you think they have said by summarising and saying, for example: *'So, let me see if I've got this right ...'*
- Ask the other person to summarise what they think you have agreed at the end of a discussion – this saves misunderstanding, so often a major factor when relationships break down

FEATURES OF SUCCESSFUL RELATIONSHIPS

SELF-FOCUS
SELF-AWARENESS

Understanding how you come across to others, and the impact your behaviour has on them, puts you in the driving seat. By this I mean that when you are interacting with other people you will make better-informed decisions about what style, process and skills to use with people in your relationship network.

People with well-developed self-awareness:

- Understand the impact they have on others
- Recognise their own strengths and weaknesses
- Ask others for feedback
- Create a positive impression

- Respond constructively to feedback
- Demonstrate the ability to reflect and adapt
- Know their own capabilities

> *'I think self-awareness is probably the most important thing towards being a champion.'*
> **Billie Jean King (Tennis player)**

FEATURES OF SUCCESSFUL RELATIONSHIPS

SELF-FOCUS

SELF-AWARENESS

Improving your self-awareness is largely about receiving and understanding feedback from others, then using this feedback to understand the impact you have on others. So:

- Ask for feedback – start with people you trust, whose opinions you value

- Be specific – say what you want feedback on, eg: *'Can you please give me some feedback on my body language and its impact on you?'*

- Listen to the feedback and ask questions to clarify and ensure you understand

- If the feedback is inconsistent with your self-perception, don't discount it – ask other people

- **Don't try to justify** your behaviour – listen and understand. If you discount what people say, they will be less likely to give you feedback in the future

- Review your skills regularly by taking part in training courses and completing self-assessment inventories that will help you to understand more about yourself

- Listen to loved ones and friends – their perspective of your personality may differ from that of people you work with

FEATURES OF SUCCESSFUL RELATIONSHIPS

FOCUS ON OTHERS
AWARENESS OF OTHERS

So far the focus has been on awareness of your own qualities and their impact on others. Observing and reading other people and assessing their responses to you and the messages they are conveying will help make you even more relationship savvy. Good powers of observation and analysis are vital here.

Someone with a good awareness of others:

- Shows interest in and gets along with people from different backgrounds
- Adapts behaviour to suit situation and person
- Makes self available to others
- Is approachable on a day to day basis
- Is comfortable and confident with other people
- Observes and reads other people's behaviour

> *'O wad some power the giftie gie us to see oursels as ithers see us!'*
> **Robert Burns from 'To a Louse' (Scottish poet, 1759-1796)**

FEATURES OF SUCCESSFUL RELATIONSHIPS

FOCUS ON OTHERS

AWARENESS OF OTHERS

Being aware of the messages other people convey in their behaviour, and knowing how to interpret these messages, will have a huge impact on the way you relate to others. By recognising and responding to the clues people give you about their moods, feelings, emotions and thoughts, you will be more likely to relate to them in a way that benefits the relationship overall. Here are some tips that will help you:

- Be genuinely curious about other people – ask questions to help you understand who they really are

- Observe those in your relationship network so that you become familiar with their behaviour and can begin to 'read' them. Recognise the habitual cues and clues they give you

- Focus on people's good qualities. This doesn't mean ignoring their deficiencies, but it does give you a better chance of being positive rather than negative in the relationship

- Get out and about and meet others in their work area – manage by walking about – that way you see more of the real person

FEATURES OF SUCCESSFUL RELATIONSHIPS

FOCUS ON OTHERS
BUILDING TRUST

Without trust a relationship is pretty sterile; with trust relationships can be truly mutually beneficial. Trust involves reliability, responsibility and dependability. It takes time to develop yet it can be lost in a breath.

To encourage others to trust you:

- Demonstrate your reliability by following through
- Keep others updated on progress
- Keep your promises
- Take responsibility for actions and outcomes
- Demonstrate consistency in action and behaviour
- Treat others fairly

> *'The chief lesson I have learned in a long life is that the only way to make a man trustworthy is to trust him; and the surest way to make him untrustworthy is to distrust him and show your distrust.'*
> **Henry L. Stimson (US politician, 1867-1950)**

FOCUS ON OTHERS

BUILDING TRUST

Trust, once broken, signals the end of a relationship, making restoration an uphill challenge for both parties. So:

DO	DON'T
✔ Be genuine	✘ Gossip about people
✔ Fulfil your responsibilities	✘ Tell lies
✔ Right wrongs quickly	✘ Fake sincerity or interest
✔ Use discretion	✘ Let people down on their expectations
✔ Ask others for feedback	✘ Avoid saying sorry!
✔ Demonstrate 'real' interest in people	✘ Make promises you can't keep
✔ Show appreciation	

> *'Real integrity is doing the right thing, knowing that nobody's going to know whether you did it or not.'*
> **Oprah Winfrey (US TV personality)**

FEATURES OF SUCCESSFUL RELATIONSHIPS

FOCUS ON OTHERS

RAPPORT & EMPATHY

Building rapport is about creating connections with people, making links and bonding, all of which helps with relationship development. Without rapport it is difficult to get beyond either a casual or transactional relationship.

People who are good at building rapport and displaying empathy put others at ease from the outset, and connect with them in a personal and genuine manner. They are aware of, and respond to, other people's emotions, often picking up non-verbal signals. They also have the ability to see issues and situations from the other person's perspective.

> *'Some people think only intellect counts: knowing how to solve problems, knowing how to get by, knowing how to identify an advantage and seize it. But the functions of intellect are insufficient without courage, love, friendship, compassion and empathy.'*
> **Dean Koontz (Author)**

FEATURES OF SUCCESSFUL RELATIONSHIPS

FOCUS ON OTHERS

RAPPORT & EMPATHY

There are simple techniques that are easy to practise to help you demonstrate and develop rapport. It is also easy, however, to appear insincere if you overplay your hand. So try out some of the techniques below and ask others for feedback on how you come across.

- Use the person's name
- Show interest in the whole person
- Match your voice and body language to the person with whom you are communicating
- Pace yourself to match him or her (eg speed of speech)
- Find something you have in common
- Spend time getting to know about the other person
- Ask questions to get them talking
- Maintain appropriate eye contact

FOCUS ON OTHERS

RAPPORT & EMPATHY

Empathy is not sympathy – it is about understanding the other person's position, not just sympathising. It also involves showing compassion. You need to develop the ability to empathise if you want to build mature mutually dependent relationships in which both parties feel equally valued and understood.

- Take time to listen to others and to understand what makes them feel the way they do

- Show that you recognise how they might be feeling: *'I sense that you are frustrated'*.

- Check that you understand why – either by asking: *'What is making you feel like this?'* or offering your thoughts: *'Is it because no one is listening to your point of view?'*

- Learn to recognise, differentiate and talk about different emotional states

- Be prepared to talk an emotional language, ie be able to report on the emotions you experience both in yourself and others

- Observe people to understand how they demonstrate their emotions – reading others will help you to respond appropriately and thus with empathy

FOCUS ON OTHERS
EMOTIONAL AWARENESS

Many people find it difficult to recognise their emotions; naming and sharing them is even harder. The ability both to understand your own feelings and to talk about them will pay dividends in relationship management, as will the practice of noticing and reacting to the feelings of others. Like many other relationship skills, however, this requires work.

Emotionally aware people are willing to talk about their own emotions. They are quick to recognise what they feel when relating to others and ensure that they do not allow their judgement to be clouded by an over-emotional response. Their emotional maturity shows in their sensitivity and responsiveness to other people; they encourage self-disclosure and are good at interpreting others' feelings.

> *'I feel guilty when people say I'm the greatest on the scene. What's good or bad doesn't matter to me; what does matter is feeling and not feeling. If only people would take more of a true view and think in terms of feelings. Your name doesn't mean a damn, it's your talents and feelings that matter. You've got to know much more than just the technicalities of notes; you've got to know what goes between the notes.'*
> **Jimi Hendrix (US rock musician and singer, 1942-1970)**

FOCUS ON OTHERS

EMOTIONAL AWARENESS

Any event or situation will trigger feelings and in order to develop your skill in this area it is necessary to be able to name the emotion you are experiencing. Here's a list (it's not exhaustive!):

Good feelings –
confident, amazed, happy, joyful, delighted, optimistic, surprised, serene, lucky, relaxed, courageous, excited, passionate, enthusiastic, optimistic, touched, loved, fascinated, cheerful, thrilled, sure, peaceful, content, co-operative

Difficult feelings –
frustrated, sad, annoyed, aggressive, guilty, sceptical, confused, embarrassed, miserable, unsure, unhappy, disillusioned, furious, hesitant, upset, lonely, afraid, nervous, belittled, irritated, despondent, distressed, alone, ignored

FEATURES OF SUCCESSFUL RELATIONSHIPS

FOCUS ON OTHERS
EMOTIONAL AWARENESS

An emotion is a message to be understood; understanding it raises your awareness of why you feel the way you do. Practise identifying your feelings in a variety of situations by:

- Putting a name to the feeling
- Identify what it is telling you about the situation
- Asking yourself why you feel this way

It will help to be aware of how you demonstrate this feeling to others. Does your body language or voice change? Do you verbalise the feeling?

Reflect on how your expression of emotions affects others:

- How do you rate your own awareness of other people's feelings when interacting?
- Do you notice easily or is it a challenge?
- What do you notice about others when they express their feelings? Is there a change in body language or voice? Do they tell you how they feel, ie name the feeling?
- Try asking: *'How does this make you feel?'* or *'What are you feeling right now?'* You never know, they might be happy to tell you and pleased that you asked

FOCUS ON OTHERS

EMOTIONAL MANAGEMENT

Having established that it is good to understand your emotions and learn to express them, the next step is being able to manage your responses. Understanding your emotional behaviour and learning how to channel your feelings appropriately can significantly improve your capability in many relationship situations.

Emotional management involves:

- Demonstrating awareness of your own emotions
- Regulating your own emotional behaviour when responding to others
- Controlling your emotions when necessary
- Acting appropriately to your own emotional responses
- Adjusting your behaviour to meet other people's needs
- Appreciating the impact of your own emotions on others

'Men decide far more problems by hate, love, lust, rage, sorrow, joy, hope, fear, illusion, or some other inward emotion, than by reality, authority, any legal standard, judicial precedent, or statute.'
Cicero (Roman author, orator and politician, 106 BC-43 BC)

FOCUS ON OTHERS

EMOTIONAL MANAGEMENT

Demonstrating and developing emotional management involves reflection and analysis, and can only be achieved if you focus on your own real life emotional reactions.

- Focus on your emotional reaction to different people and situations and name the emotions you experience

- Identify any patterns that emerge:
  - By type of person
  - By type of situation
  - By the emotion you are experiencing

- Ask yourself why you might have this response. What triggers it?

- Explore, in a cool, calm and collected way, how you might respond/deal with these people/situations more effectively

FEATURES OF SUCCESSFUL RELATIONSHIPS

FOCUS ON OTHERS
MUTUAL RESPECT

Our final quality, mutual respect, is the basis of many effective relationships. Without respect a relationship is likely to falter and slowly die. Many of the characteristics of this feature of good relationships involve basic manners and common sense – sadly not always as common as one would like.

A person who shows respect:

- Is polite and well mannered in interactions with others
- Is attentive when communicating
- Uses appropriate demeanour
- Encourages contribution from others
- Welcomes others' opinions
- Appreciates the importance of own and others' dignity
- Responds to others' needs in an appropriate way

> *'If you want to be respected, you must respect yourself.'*
> **(Spanish proverb)**

FEATURES OF SUCCESSFUL RELATIONSHIPS

FOCUS ON OTHERS
MUTUAL RESPECT

To demonstrate and develop mutual respect:

- Treat others as you would wish to be treated yourself
- Be responsive – stay on topic and respond clearly and directly to what people say
- Ask others how they feel before making decisions that affect them
- Don't interrupt
- Be willing to explore topics fully, especially when you have different perspectives. Accept the difference and show you understand even if you don't agree
- Respect others' points of view, ask questions to gain a full picture of the other person's perspective and demonstrate you understand their position
- Be non judgemental – accept people as they are, not as you would want them to be!
- Be tough on the issues not on the people

FOCUS ON OTHERS
MUTUAL RESPECT

It is also worth remembering that people tend to feel disrespected when:

- They feel judged and rejected
- Not listened to
- Laughed at
- Not taken seriously
- Their privacy is invaded
- Others believe they know what is best for them and tell them
- Not asked for their ideas
- Stereotyped

FEATURES OF SUCCESSFUL RELATIONSHIPS

PERSONAL SKILLS AUDIT

Using the descriptions on the previous pages, assess your own needs and skills level in relation to each of the features of successful relationships. (1 = not important, 5 = very important)

Relationship Skill – Self-focus	Level of importance for me in relationships at work *(level 1 – 5)*	My current skill level with my relationships at work *(level 1 – 5)*
Assertiveness		
Communication skills		
Caring and supporting		
Honesty and integrity		
Listening and questioning		
Self-awareness		

FEATURES OF SUCCESSFUL RELATIONSHIPS

PERSONAL SKILLS AUDIT

Relationship Skill – Focus on Others	Level of importance for me in relationships at work (level 1 – 5)	My current skill level with my relationships at work (level 1 – 5)
Awareness of others		
Building trust		
Rapport and empathy		
Emotional awareness		
Emotional management		
Mutual respect		

PERSONAL SKILLS AUDIT

ANALYSIS

Analyse your responses to the skills audit and identify:

- Your strengths and weaknesses
- Why you believe certain skills are more important than others
- Skills you want to develop and how you intend to develop them

CASE STUDY 3 – CARMEN & JAMES

Carmen and James had been part of the same project team for four years. They'd always worked well together and had a friendly yet challenging relationship.

They both had different strengths and weaknesses. James tended to be more creative and innovative while Carmen was very organised and structured. Their weaknesses were that James left things to the last minute and appeared completely disorganised while Carmen was impatient and could seem over-controlling.

Both liked to get their own way but they had realised that they were better as a double act than on their own. Over the years they had developed a good social and work based mutually dependent relationship. They tended to seek one another out to share new ideas and to discuss challenges and problems.

FEATURES OF SUCCESSFUL RELATIONSHIPS

CASE STUDY 3 – CARMEN & JAMES

Trust and openness were key features of their relationship and this allowed them to challenge one another and, at times, to agree to differ.

However, after three years the relationship faced a challenge when James was promoted to Project Leader, with Carmen reporting to him. Initially this caused a slight blip in their relationship. Carmen became more guarded, fearing that their previous open, honest and frank relationship was no longer appropriate. She was concerned that the change in role might mean that James would now see her behaviour as disrespectful and this could ultimately affect her career.

James noticed the changes in Carmen's behaviour and was quick to instigate an informal meeting. He invited her out for lunch and spent time explaining that while his role had changed, he hadn't. Although he was her boss, and in certain situations boss-like behaviour might be necessary, he wanted them to continue to have the quality of mutually dependent relationship that they had previously enjoyed.

CASE STUDY

FEATURES OF SUCCESSFUL RELATIONSHIPS

CASE STUDY 3 – CARMEN & JAMES
CARMEN & JAMES' ACTION POINTS

Fortunately, the quality of the relationship prior to James's promotion had a sufficiently strong basis for their former working partnership to be restored.

Their action points:

- To recognise that any variation in the basis of a relationship causes changes in the perception of the relationship

- Regular behaviour modelling by James to put Carmen at ease

- For James to talk individually to the rest of the project team to find out if other members were also having problems with his new status

- To make use of the **skilful dialogue technique** (see toolkit, final chapter) to ensure that the quality of their previously successful relationship is maintained, and the **observation technique** to be aware of any changes and ready to respond speedily and appropriately. This will help avoid any future misunderstandings or another breakdown in the relationship

WHAT MAKES RELATIONSHIPS <u>UNSUCCESSFUL</u>

FINDING A WAY

Some relationships go wrong from the start – perhaps one can say they never get started! Other relationships deteriorate slowly and some come to a sudden end.

Whatever the reason for an unsuccessful work based relationship, the long term impact can be demotivating, demoralising and frustrating for both parties.

One of my former bosses used to say to me: *'I don't need you to like them, I just need you to work with them!'* This is a concept worth reflecting on – you cannot like all of the people you work with all of the time. The issue is finding a way to work together constructively.

WHAT MAKES RELATIONSHIPS UNSUCCESSFUL

MISUNDERSTANDING

When asked, people give a variety of reasons for relationships going wrong or being unsuccessful (see the model overleaf). There are, however, two reasons that are worthy of special mention as they are referred to so frequently. They are **being let down** and **misunderstanding**.

When asked for clarification, people say things like:

- *'Broken promises'*
- *'When people feel you have let them down even about petty things'*
- *'Lack of understanding of needs and requirements'*
- *'Not following through'*
- *'Forgetting what they promised'*

These two reasons are not surprising in themselves as causes of relationship problems, but they are not necessarily the ones you'd expect to see heading the list, ahead of terms like bullying, lack of consideration, people being dishonest, manipulative or distant. On reflection, people may feel that the latter qualities prevent relationships from existing in the first place!

WHAT MAKES RELATIONSHIPS UNSUCCESSFUL

10 FACTORS

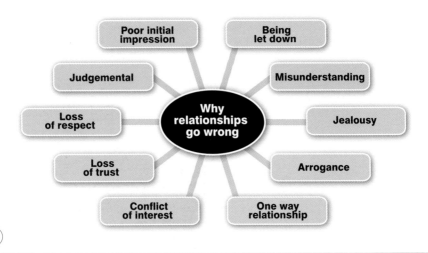

Poor initial impression

Being let down

Judgemental

Misunderstanding

Loss of respect

Why relationships go wrong

Jealousy

Loss of trust

Arrogance

Conflict of interest

One way relationship

DEVELOPING COPING STRATEGIES

The 10 factors listed are fairly self-explanatory and their negative effects on relationships do not need further explanation. The issue is that while most of us would naturally choose to make relationships and work with people who make us feel good, this is not always possible. There will be times for all of us when we have to deal with people who don't make us feel so good – people who are manipulative, inconsiderate, distant or worse.

What we need to be able to do is to develop ways of coping with these relationships to make them as effective as possible. There is no one perfect answer. **The challenge is to find the most appropriate way for you**.

WHAT MAKES RELATIONSHIPS UNSUCCESSFUL

DEVELOPING COPING STRATEGIES

Possible approaches include:

- Learn to ignore what annoys you and get on with it – remember, you can't like all of the people all of the time
- If you are brave, try talking to them about how they make you feel and how you believe you could best work with them to ensure effective outcomes
- Adapt your behaviour, deal with the situation/person and move on
- Work through or with a third party who can help the process
- Look on the interaction as a development opportunity!
- Ponder your own annoying habits

CASE STUDY 4 – JOCELYN & AMANDA

Jocelyn had worked quite closely with fellow consultant Amanda on several projects over many months and from the start had found the relationship challenging and testing.

Jocelyn, 32, had joined the organisation seven months ago from another consultancy and was on a fast track programme.

Amanda, 52, had been with the organisation for eight years and her career had grown with the company. She was now in a senior consultancy role, was highly regarded and excellent at her job.

C
A
S
E

S
T
U
D
Y

CASE STUDY 4 – JOCELYN & AMANDA

Amanda appeared to have taken a dislike to Jocelyn. Nothing particularly unpleasant had happened, but there were constant small snubs. It seemed that she:

- Didn't listen to or take account of Jocelyn's ideas
- Ignored her in big gatherings
- Didn't bring her into discussions
- Made occasional snide comments, eg *'of course we're not all lucky enough to be fast tracked',* and, *'maybe our new girl has some thoughts she'd like to share'*

C
A
S
E

S
T
U
D
Y

CASE STUDY 4 – JOCELYN & AMANDA

Initially Jocelyn did not understand why Amanda didn't like her. She thought she had done nothing out of the ordinary to cause such a reaction. We discussed Jocelyn's view of Amanda's relationship style:

- What was important to her
- What motivated her
- What demotivated her
- Who were her 'friends' at work

It appeared that Amanda was quite introverted, keeping herself to herself. She was confident of her own abilities but had little need for social relationships at work. Using the relationship model we identified that she tended to have casual and transactional relationships with people. Jocelyn, on the other hand, wanted more social and mutually dependent relationships. Perhaps this was one of the issues.

C
A
S
E

S
T
U
D
Y

CASE STUDY 4 – JOCELYN & AMANDA

Jocelyn was becoming increasingly dissatisfied with the situation – she simply wasn't sure what she had done wrong. This was when she decided to get some help and attended our training course. During the programme we reviewed the actions she had already taken to try to improve the situation. They were:

- Offering to work on projects with Amanda to learn from her
- Asking Amanda's opinion before offering her own ideas
- Building on and supporting Amanda's ideas and plans
- Increasingly, keeping quiet when in meetings with Amanda to avoid conflict
- Avoiding working with her as much as possible (not easy because they worked in the same business group)

These are all sound strategies to try when attempting to discover what's going wrong in a relationship and aiming to get it back on track.

CASE STUDY 4 – JOCELYN & AMANDA

Jocelyn also admitted that she had probably 'upset' Amanda early on by talking too much about her previous job and the relevance of her previous experience to some of their joint projects. This led to a discussion about how Amanda might perceive Jocelyn. We identified several themes that might be affecting the relationship, or at least Jocelyn's perception of it, and agreed some plans of action.

Themes

- Their different perceptions of work based relationships
- Jocelyn's apparent arrogance and overconfidence (in Amanda's eyes)
- (Possibly) Jocelyn's youth and confident manner

**C
A
S
E

S
T
U
D
Y**

CASE STUDY 4 – JOCELYN & AMANDA
JOCELYN'S ACTION POINTS

- To recognise that people have different needs in work based relationships
- To continue to play down her previous experience and fast track role
- When appropriate, to ask Amanda for her opinion on issues relating to projects and processes
- To ask Amanda for a formal meeting to review how they are working together on their joint projects. This would give Jocelyn the opportunity to express some of her worries and explore ways, with Amanda, of making their relationship workable
- To join her for lunch or a coffee occasionally, to try to develop a more mutually satisfying relationship, accepting that Amanda's needs in this area differ from Jocelyn's

From the toolkit, aspects of **skilful dialogue, appreciative focus** and **feedback** may prove useful in dealing with this situation.

We agreed that Jocelyn might have to accept that this would never be a mutually dependent relationship, but that if she worked at it, she could certainly improve the current situation.

C
A
S
E

S
T
U
D
Y

THE RELATIONSHIP TOOLKIT

THE RELATIONSHIP TOOLKIT

THE TOOLS

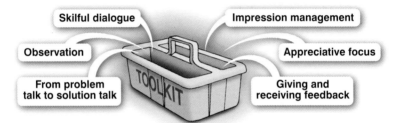

Skilful dialogue

Impression management

Observation

Appreciative focus

From problem talk to solution talk

Giving and receiving feedback

This relationship toolkit suggests some ideas that could prove useful to you in your relationship management and development. Each of these ideas can stand alone or, alternatively, elements of each one can be combined.

I suggest trying first those ideas that fit best with your own style and personality, and become comfortable and confident using those before moving on to others. If a technique doesn't work first time, don't give up; try it again on someone else or in a different situation.

THE RELATIONSHIP TOOLKIT

SKILFUL DIALOGUE

Good quality dialogue between people is the basis of all relationships. Dialogue is a conversation between people, involving the exchange and exploration of thoughts and ideas. It sounds simple, so why is it difficult with some people?

When dialogue is difficult there are a few major reasons:

- Personality issues
- Misunderstanding
- Differences of opinion
- Style differences
- Time constraints
- Stereotyping
- Differences of perception regarding either the issue or the people
- Game playing by one of the parties

> *'I see people in terms of dialogue and I believe that people are their talk.'*
> **Roddy Doyle (Irish novelist, b 1958)**

THE RELATIONSHIP TOOLKIT

SKILFUL DIALOGUE

Skilful dialogue is a combination of two of the features of successful relationships – **communication** and **listening and questioning** – and involves structured use of these features. You can use this process in many challenging situations as a way of keeping things objective and focusing on the issue, while engaging in dialogue to maintain the relationship.

To maintain dialogue there are a few simple rules to follow:

- Give the other person your full attention – always easier with people you like and respect
- Demonstrate you are listening by:
  - A good level of eye contact
  - Using *mmm, yes*, head nods, etc to indicate you are on track
  - Asking questions to fully explore the issue under discussion
  - Summarising to make sure you understand fully and to show the other person you have understood their perspective
  - Sticking to the point

THE RELATIONSHIP TOOLKIT

SKILFUL DIALOGUE

- State your own views, position or ideas clearly and concisely
- Try to establish links to and build on the other person's ideas
- If you disagree say so, explain why and allow for further discussion
- Focus on the issue under discussion, not on the person and your views of them – especially if it is someone you find challenging to deal with

The important issue here is to keep an open mind, keep channels of communication open and keep talking. In his book *'The Seven Habits of Highly Effective People'*, Steven Covey suggests:

> *'Seek first to understand then to be understood.'*

This is a good rule to follow. Don't we all feel better when we believe that we have been listened to and understood?

THE RELATIONSHIP TOOLKIT

IMPRESSION MANAGEMENT

What is impression management? It is the effect you have on others; it is about ensuring that you give yourself the best possible opportunity to create a positive and lasting impression. Like it or not, impression is often based on the initial impact you make and then the subsequent feeling that you leave others with.

Where relationships are concerned impression management is vital – both creating and maintaining it. In his book *'Personal Impact'*, Michael Shea says:

> *'When we see someone for the first time, the initial sound/visual 'bite' – a combination of their looks, their dress, their bearing and the tenor of their opening remarks – become deeply etched in our minds and affect our attitudes to them!'*

THE RELATIONSHIP TOOLKIT

IMPRESSION MANAGEMENT

Building a positive and lasting impression is a complex process of using the appropriate:

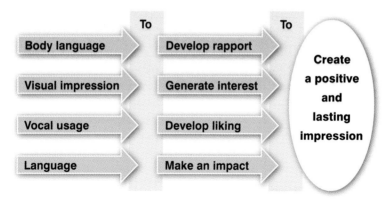

	To		To	
Body language		Develop rapport		
Visual impression		Generate interest		Create a positive and lasting impression
Vocal usage		Develop liking		
Language		Make an impact		

THE RELATIONSHIP TOOLKIT

IMPRESSION MANAGEMENT

Impression management is particularly useful in the early days of a relationship when you need to establish your credentials and credibility. That said, being aware of the impression you are creating is valuable in any interpersonal situation.

The various elements of impression management involve:

- Body language – eye contact, gestures, posture and facial impression
- Visual impression – dress, appearance, distinctiveness, memorability
- Vocal usage – intonation, pace, pitch, rhythm, accent
- Language – use of words, no jargon, clear expression
- Rapport – find a common link, establish similarities, begin to build trust
- Interest – keep information relevant and make your listeners curious
- Liking – demonstrate your interest in them, be sincere, make them want to talk to YOU
- Impact – try out new techniques, be different, make it memorable

Note: for more on this area see the *'Impact & Presence Pocketbook'*.

THE RELATIONSHIP TOOLKIT

APPRECIATIVE FOCUS

The process of Appreciative Inquiry (AI) has been used successfully for many years to bring about change in organisational development. The key principles of AI have been adapted, enabling you to take an appreciative focus in your relationship management and development.

The basis of the approach is to discover what brings about success rather than failure. When using it for relationship development it is largely about asking questions to recognise the best in people and to identify new potential and possibilities. AI is typically used where a previously successful relationship has broken down and needs mending, or where a group of people are collectively in a negative state of mind and you want to encourage them to reflect on better times, in order to change their mood and move on.

By discovering the best in people through asking positive questions you can *'apprehend, anticipate and heighten positive potential'* (Cooperrider, 2003).

THE RELATIONSHIP TOOLKIT

APPRECIATIVE FOCUS

There are five common methods of using an appreciative focus in your relationship management and development:

1. Focus on the positive in inquiry – asking questions to determine what is working now or has worked so far.

2. Encourage people to tell stories in detail about what has worked for them.

3. Identify the positive themes that emerge and begin to develop ways of building on these themes.

4. Work together to plan for a positive way of working in the future.

5. Constantly review progress to build on the positive and truly develop an appreciative environment.

APPRECIATIVE FOCUS

Here's an example of this approach:

1. Questions – What do we like about working with each other? Anything else?

2. Story – Thinking about the last time we enjoyed working together, let's describe what went well.

3. Themes – Let's name the things we enjoy and plan how we can build on these.

4. Action Plan – A joint plan to explore ways to work together positively and appreciatively.

5. Review – Two-way review to gain feedback and build on the positives.

THE RELATIONSHIP TOOLKIT

FROM PROBLEM TALK TO SOLUTION TALK

This approach aims to transform our usual way of dealing with relationship issues by focusing on solutions **not** problems. It emerged from the therapeutic world in the 1980s and has been applied in a variety of management and leadership areas since then.

When used as part of the relationship toolkit, solution talk involves:

- Working with what people **can** do rather than what they can't!
- Focusing on what people find helpful and how this can be built on
- Asking questions rather than suggesting answers
- Listening, to establish reinforcing messages
- Identifying details of solutions not problems
- Raising awareness of and focusing on success
- Encouraging commitment to moving towards a solution

This technique is useful if you have reached an impasse when working with others and the relationship is in danger of breaking down. Either by applying solution talk to yourself, or by employing it with others, you can focus on what's going well. With this in mind, what small steps can you begin to take to move towards better outcomes?

THE RELATIONSHIP TOOLKIT

FROM PROBLEM TALK TO SOLUTION TALK

The more you practise solution talk with other people, the easier it becomes to apply it to yourself. Try some of these ideas:

Support the other person in your initial response by showing you understand that things may be difficult

Open up the discussion to explore times when they have successfully dealt with a similar situation

Listen for evidence of strengths and approaches they have used in the past to solve similar challenges and point this out to them

Understand and explore what they have already done to deal with the problem

Talk to them about the future and what it will feel like when things are better

Interrupt if necessary to stop problem talk and move to solution talk

Offer positive feedback indicating your support for ideas to take things forward

Notice their emotional state and feelings expressed and respond accordingly

Suggest they identify small steps which will take them towards a better outcome

THE RELATIONSHIP TOOLKIT

GIVING & RECEIVING FEEDBACK

Feedback is an under-utilised skill, yet one that is fundamental for successful relationship development. Open, supportive relationships depend on a person's ability both to give and receive feedback. Here are some tips:

Giving feedback to others:

- Focus on actions and behaviour and give examples – *'When you … it makes me feel...'*
- Comment on why the behaviour or action affected you the way it did, whether it is positive or negative
- Balance praise and constructive criticism
- Give the person a chance to respond, ask questions and explore
- Listen to their response and demonstrate understanding of their reaction – delving deeper if necessary
- Give feedback in a timely manner – as soon after an event/interaction as possible
- Make sure the environment is appropriate, eg don't give feedback in the middle of an open plan office

THE RELATIONSHIP TOOLKIT

GIVING & RECEIVING FEEDBACK

Receiving feedback from others:

- Ask an open question about an aspect of your behaviour or performance
- Ask someone you trust and respect: you will value the feedback more!
- Clarify to ensure you understand
- Acknowledge any valid points
- Don't get defensive (even if you feel it); think about the feedback and why the person has given it
- Thank the person for their feedback and if appropriate indicate how you will use it in future interactions

Giving and receiving feedback is a particularly useful tool when someone is giving you a hard time or when you know you are in danger of 'falling out' over something relatively trivial. The key to success in using this technique is to build it into your day to day relationship management approach and **to remember that it is a two-way process**.

THE RELATIONSHIP TOOLKIT

GIVING & RECEIVING FEEDBACK

Two thoughts about feedback that are worth remembering:

'We judge ourselves by our intentions and others by their actions'

And

'I can't tell you what you are and you can't tell me what I see'

The success of the feedback process rests with the person giving feedback adopting appropriate behaviour and the recipient understanding, reflecting and acting on the feedback.

THE RELATIONSHIP TOOLKIT

OBSERVATION

Developing and mastering the art of observing others, together with the ability to read situations, can be very useful in relationships. Research has shown that in face to face communication, when people are involved in emotional conversations, up to 93% of the impact of a message is non verbal (Mehrabian, 1981). If one accepts this, then skill in the area of reading and recognising the signs displayed by people in social and interpersonal situations will help you to become more effective in managing your relationships.

Observation involves using both eyes and ears to monitor people and situations, eg:

- Watching other people's facial expressions, eye contact levels, body movements, postures and gestures

- Listening to people and the way they communicate – their vocal tones, pitch, speed, use of silence and pauses

- Observing the interactions between people, who talks to whom and who ignores whom

- Observing the situation, surroundings and environment for cues and clues

THE RELATIONSHIP TOOLKIT

OBSERVATION

Observation takes practice and patience. Here are a few tips to hone your skills:

- Slow down and take time to watch others
- Pay close attention to your physical surroundings: who, what, when, where and how
- Start by practising with familiar surroundings, people and situations
- Watch for clusters of behaviour
- In meetings, try to identify people's verbal and non verbal behaviour, their communication style and idiosyncrasies – to help you communicate better with them during the meeting and in the future
- Become aware of and note people's reactions, emotions, and motivations
- Practise by observing what is around you: for instance, when out for a walk or at a busy location, eg a shopping mall, or airport, stop and take notice. At some point later that day try to recall what you saw

Becoming a people watcher and applying these processes to your own relationship network will give you an edge in terms of recognising people's behaviour, habits and patterns. This will help you to identify any changes and be more capable of responding appropriately.

WORKING RELATIONSHIPS

AND FINALLY

I have always believed that my time has been wisely invested when developing and maintaining my relationships at work. For that reason I agree wholeheartedly with Margaret Wheatley's quote, taken from *Leadership and the New Science:*

> *'In organisations, real power and energy is generated through relationships.'*

I do hope that this short pocketbook helps **you** to get the most from your work based relationships.

FURTHER INFORMATION

REFERENCES

Myers-Briggs Type Indicator® (MBTI®) available in the UK from Oxford Psychologists Press.

Relationship Awareness Theory – Elias Porter and the Strength Deployment Inventory® (SDI®) available in the UK from Personal Strengths UK

Social Style Model™ by Tracom Group™

7 Habits of Highly Effective People, Stephen R Covey, Simon & Schuster, 1989

Impact & Presence Pocketbook, Pam Jones & Janie Van Hool, Management Pocketbooks Ltd, 2004

Silent Messages: Implicit Communication of Emotions and Attitudes, Albert Mehrabian, Wadsworth Publishing, 1981

Assertiveness Pocketbook, Max A Eggert, Management Pocketbooks Ltd, 1997

Communicator's Pocketbook, Seán Mistéil, Management Pocketbooks Ltd, 1997

READING LIST

Appreciative Inquiry Handbook, David L. Cooperrider, Diana Whitney, & Jacqueline M. Stavros, Berrett-Koehler, 2008

Emotional Intelligence: Why It Can Matter More Than IQ, Daniel Goleman, Bloomsbury Publishing, 1996

Peoplesmart: Developing Your Interpersonal Intelligence, Mel Silberman, Berrett-Koehler, 2000

People Styles At Work: Making Bad Relationships Good and Good Relationships Better, Robert Bolton & Dorothy Grover Bolton, AMACOM, 1996

Social Intelligence: The New Science of Human Relationships, Daniel Goleman, Arrow Books Ltd, 2007

Social Intelligence: The New Science of Success, Karl Albrecht, Jossey Bass, 2006

The Solutions Focus: The Simple Way to Positive Change, Paul Z. Jackson & Mark McKergow, Nicholas Brealey Publishing, 2002

Thin Book of Appreciative Inquiry, Sue Annis Hammond, St Luke's Innovative Resources, 1996

Working Relationships: The Simple Truth About Getting Along With Friends and Foes at Work, B. Wall, Davies Black, 1999

About the Author

Fiona Dent
Fiona works at Ashridge Business School where she is a Director of Executive Education. She has over 20 years' experience in the management development business and prior to joining Ashridge she held various management development positions in financial services organisations.

Fiona teaches, coaches, researches and consults in the areas of influencing, interpersonal skills, leadership, lifelong learning and personal skills development. She is the author of several books including *The Leadership Pocketbook* and *The Self-managed Development Pocketbook*.

Contact
In addition to her work at Ashridge Fiona also runs her own consultancy and can be contacted at:
Fiona.Dent@ashridge.org.uk

Your details

Name _____

Position _____

Company _____

Address _____

_____

Telephone _____

Fax _____

E-mail _____

VAT No. (EC companies) _____

Your Order Ref _____

Please send me:

	No. copies
The Working Relationships _____ Pocketbook	[ ]
The _____ Pocketbook	[ ]
The _____ Pocketbook	[ ]
The _____ Pocketbook	[ ]

Order by Post
MANAGEMENT POCKETBOOKS LTD
LAUREL HOUSE, STATION APPROACH,
ALRESFORD, HAMPSHIRE SO24 9JH UK
Order by Phone, Fax or Internet
Telephone: +44 (0)1962 735573
Facsimile: +44 (0)1962 733637
E-mail: sales@pocketbook.co.uk
Web: www.pocketbook.co.uk

Customers in USA should contact:
Management Pocketbooks
2427 Bond Street, University Park, IL 60466
Telephone: 866 620 6944 Facsimile: 708 534 7803
E-mail: mp.orders@ware-pak.com
Web: www.managementpocketbooks.com